My State
NEW JERSEY

By Christina Earley

TABLE OF CONTENTS

A Crabtree Seedlings Book

Crabtree Publishing

crabtreebooks.com

School-to-Home Support for Caregivers and Teachers

This book helps children grow by letting them practice reading. Here are a few guiding questions to help the reader build his or her comprehension skills. Possible answers appear in red.

Before Reading:

- What do I know about New Jersey?
    - *I know that New Jersey is a state.*
    - *I know that New Jersey has cold and snowy winters.*

- What do I want to learn about New Jersey?
    - *I want to learn which famous people were born in New Jersey.*
    - *I want to learn what the state flag looks like.*

During Reading:

- What have I learned so far?
    - *I have learned that Trenton is the state capital of New Jersey.*
    - *I have learned that the first blueberry crop in the U.S. was grown at Whitesbog.*

- I wonder why...
    - *I wonder why the state flower is the common blue violet.*
    - *I wonder why Cape May is a national historic landmark.*

After Reading:

- What did I learn about New Jersey?
    - *I have learned that you can swim at Ocean City beach.*
    - *I have learned that the state animal is the horse.*

- Read the book again and look for the glossary words.
    - *I see the word **capital** on page 6, and the word **harvest** on page 14. The other glossary words are found on pages 22 and 23.*

NEW JERSEY

Hi! My name is Mia.
Welcome to New Jersey!
Jilly's
T-SHIRT
FACTORY
DAVID'S
DIVE SHOP
SEAPORT VILLAGE
GOLF
PIZZA

I live in Cape May. My city has many old, beautiful houses.

Cape May is a national **historic landmark**.

New Jersey is in the northeastern United States. The **capital** is Trenton.

Fun Fact: Newark is the largest city in New Jersey.

The state animal is the horse.

The common blue violet is the state flower.

We grow a lot of blueberries in New Jersey. Some of them are used to make blueberry muffins.

Fun Fact: New Jersey grows around 41 million pounds (19 million kg) of blueberries a year.

My state flag is **buff**-colored. The state **coat of arms** is in the middle.

My family and I like to watch the New Jersey Devils play hockey.

Fall is my favorite time to visit Whitesbog Historic Village. I like watching the cranberry **harvest**.

Fun Fact: The first blueberry crop in the U.S. was grown at Whitesbog.

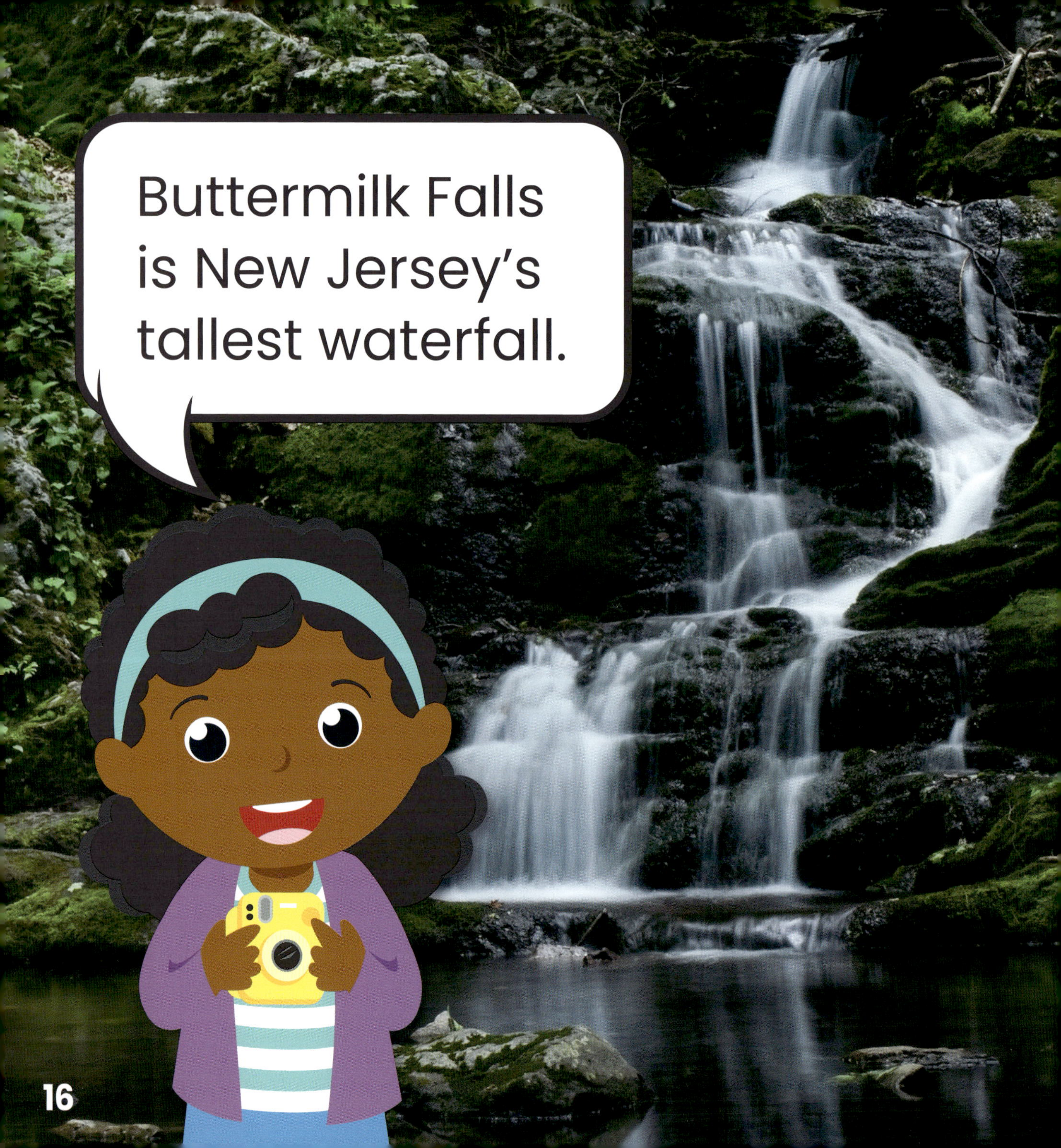
Buttermilk Falls is New Jersey's tallest waterfall.

Boating on the Hudson River is a great way to see the cliffs of the Palisades.

Singer Whitney Houston was born in New Jersey. Baseball player Mike Trout was also born in New Jersey.

Fun Fact: President Grover Cleveland was born in Caldwell, New Jersey.

Seaside Heights has some of my favorite rides!

I have fun swimming
at Ocean City beach.

Glossary

buff (buhf): A brownish-yellow color

capital (cap-ih-tuhl): The city or town where the government of a country, state, or province is located

coat of arms (coht uv armz): A special group of pictures, usually shown on a shield

harvest (har-vist): To pick and collect crops

historic (hi-stor-ik): Something that is important in history

landmark (land-mahrk): A place or building that is important in history

Index

About the Author

Christina Earley lives in sunny South Florida with her husband and son. She enjoys traveling around the United States and learning about different historical places. Her hobbies include hiking, yoga, and baking.

Written by: Christina Earley
Designed and Illustrated by: Bobbie Houser
Series Development: James Earley
Proofreader: Melissa Boyce
Educational Consultant: Marie Lemke M.Ed.

Photographs:
Newscom: Joe Robbins/Icon Sportswire 573: p. 18 right
Shutterstock: f11photo: cover; Vlad G: p. 3; EQRoy: p. 4-5, 23; Volina: p. 6, 22; Sean Pavone: p. 7; Anaite: p. 8; Predrag Lukic: p. 9; Bryan Pollard: p. 10-11; Krasula: p. 11; Joseph Sohm: p. 12, 22; Debby Wong: p. 13; Olivier Le Queinec: p. 14-15, 23; AstroStar: p. 15; Andrew F. Kazmierski: p. 16; Nate photos: p. 17; s_bukley: p. 18 left; James Kirkikis: p. 20; Gary C. Tognoni: p. 21
whitehouse.gov: p. 19

Crabtree Publishing

crabtreebooks.com 800-387-7650

Printed in the U.S.A./072023/CG20230214

Published in Canada
Crabtree Publishing
616 Welland Avenue
St. Catharines, Ontario
L2M 5V6

Published in the United States
Crabtree Publishing
347 Fifth Avenue
Suite 1402-145
New York, New York, 10016

Library and Archives Canada Cataloguing in Publication
Available at Library and Archives Canada

Library of Congress Cataloging-in-Publication Data
Available at the Library of Congress

Hardcover: 978-1-0398-0527-9
Paperback: 978-1-0398-0559-0
Ebook (pdf): 978-1-0398-0623-8
Epub: 978-1-0398-0591-0